Introvert

Discover How To Use Your Inner Strengths To Thrive And Flourish In The Modern World

By Ace McCloud
Copyright © 2014

Disclaimer

The information provided in this book is designed to provide helpful information on the subjects discussed. This book is not meant to be used, nor should it be used, to diagnose or treat any medical condition. For diagnosis or treatment of any medical problem, consult your own physician. The publisher and author are not responsible for any specific health or allergy needs that may require medical supervision and are not liable for any damages or negative consequences from any treatment, action, application or preparation, to any person reading or following the information in this book. Any references included are provided for informational purposes only. Readers should be aware that any websites or links listed in this book may change.

Table of Contents

Introduction 6

Chapter 1: How To Succeed In Challenging Situations . 8

Chapter 2: Discover Your Special Talent.....................14

Chapter 3: Determining Your Personality Type 18

Chapter 4: Utilizing Your Inner Strengths 21

Chapter 5: Making a Plan to Accomplish Your Goals...24

Conclusion...26

My Other Books and Audio Books.............................. 27

DEDICATED TO THOSE WHO ARE PLAYING THE GAME OF LIFE TO

WIN

KEEP ON PUSHING AND NEVER GIVE UP!

Ace McCloud

Be sure to check out my website for all my Books and Audio books.

www.AcesEbooks.com

Introduction

I want to thank you and congratulate you for buying the book: "Introvert: Discover How to Use Your Inner Strengths to Thrive and Flourish in the Modern World."

There are many different types of personalities, but the two most commonly known types are introversion and extroversion. Extroverts are best known for their friendly, outspoken, loud nature while introverts are best known for their preference to be alone. Approximately one or two out of every 3 people you know is an introvert.

Introversion is nothing new. The term was originally coined by Carl Jung in 1921 when he wrote his paper, "Personality Types." Jung believed that the terms introversion and extroversion were the two main personality traits of humans. Later on in 1962, a mother-daughter research team known as Myers and Briggs built upon Jung's theory by developing the Myers-Briggs Type Indicator test, which was meant to help the general public better understand personality traits. One year later, a psychologist named W.T. Norman redefined Jung, Myers and Briggs' work by suggesting that 5 factors can define a person's personality, including openness, conscientiousness, agreeableness, and introversion/extroversion.

Not much was said about introversion and extroversion again until 1999, when researchers Deborah Johnson and John Wiebe theorized that introversion and extroversion could actually be genetic. They also believed that the central blood flow of the human body had a contributing factor. Today, there are many books and publications on introversion.

Many view introversion as a negative thing. This may be due to the fact that many cultures—particularly the United States—fosters extroversion. You have probably been taught that you must be loud, outspoken and sociable to make it in today's world. While that may *seem* to be the case, the truth is that it's not. Unfortunately, many introverts believe this teaching and that can cause them to pretend to be extroverts. When an introvert is pretending to be anything but him or herself, it can prove to be unhealthy and many times people will pick up on this.

The main stereotype made about introverts is that they are shy or suffer from social phobia. Introverted people who are not aware of the true definition of their personality may find themselves believing that they are weird or that something is wrong with them. However, those are all nothing more than misconceptions. The truth is that introverts are people who are naturally quiet and spend most of their time looking inwards rather than outwards.

Sometimes, the lines between introversion and extroversion are blurred. Some people may not be one or the other but can fall somewhere in between. Are you an introvert or an extrovert? Take a minute to answer some of these questions:

- Do you prefer one-on-one conversations over groups?
- Would you rather communicate with written words than by speaking?
- Do you like to relax with yourself after spending time with others?
- Are you more focused on values than tangible possessions?
- Would you rate your listening skills as good or excellent?
- Have others told you that they admire your strong ability to focus?
- Do you prefer small gatherings over large parties?
- Are you naturally quiet or soft spoken?

If you answered yes to all or most of those questions, chances are you're an introvert, or at least mostly an introvert. If you're seeking the truth about yourself and your personality, then you've come to the right book. This book contains proven steps and strategies on how to make the most of your introverted personality. You will discover how to use your true inner strengths to your advantage to get ahead in the world without having to change who you are. First, you'll learn about the most common challenges that introvert's face and how to easily overcome them. Then you will learn about the best talents that most introverts have and what you can do to capitalize on your own personal strengths with a step-by-step action plan that you can use to put it all together. Be prepared to learn just how effective and powerful you can be when you shed the expectations of society and follow your own heart to reach your true potential!

Chapter 1: How To Succeed In Challenging Situations

"Challenges" is a word that is probably well-recognized by most introverts. The majority of extroverts find it easy to make friends, hit it off with almost anyone and they often seem to be in great jobs. They also always seem to know just what to say to get a conversation going. For introverts, most of that can seem like a crazy obstacle course. This chapter will analyze the most common challenges that introvert's face while offering solutions that can be helpful in making these challenges much easier to manage.

Friendships. Attracting friends can be a major challenge for introverts. It's not the fact that introverts don't want friends—they do—it is just more challenging for them to open up, especially in groups. If an introvert does not have a strategy for making friends easily, his or her life can easily become lonely. I have found that one of the best ways to make friends is to observe others for a while. Try to figure them out and *then* start talking to them. There will be a higher chance that they will feel more connected to you if you give off the sense that you "know" them. Another good way to try making friends is to work on your conversational skills, which you will read a little about later on this chapter. Having a good conversation starter or some good ideas to talk about can go a long way. Here are some good tips to keep in mind when it comes to friendships:

- Adapt to a social circle but don't forget to stay true to yourself.

- Try to view yourself from the outside in and imagine how others may perceive you.

- Try to differentiate between your strengths and weaknesses. For example, you may be great at making eye contact with others but when it comes to small talk you might get tongue-tied. This way you know what you should be focusing on for improvement.

- Consider taking a confidence class or read up on confidence books

Networking. Networking can be another huge barrier for introverts because groups tend to turn them off. There's nothing worse than being at a large gathering for a networking event and just shying off into the corner, especially when everyone else seems to be getting along just fine. A good solution for overcoming this challenge is to network online, since it utilizes more written communication than verbal. LinkedIn is a great website for online networking, but my personal favorite is Facebook! With just a little bit of searching around, you should be able to find some groups that you can join and work on building some friends and relationships. If you can get into or start a mastermind group on a subject that you're interested in, this will give you a major at advantage and can be very rewarding as well! It can be much easier for many people to make genuine and lasting friendships online, so be sure to put some effort into this. Here are some more tips for networking:

- Look for other people who appear to be by themselves and network one-on-one.

- Research the type of people you will be networking with if possible.

- Talk to people as friends first before you start talking about business.

- Go to a networking event with a friend.

- Use your listening skills and try to reach people that way ("Excuse me, I couldn't help but overhear that you're having trouble thinking of marketing ideas, I think I might be able to help with that...")

- Set goals that you want to achieve before you go to a networking event ("I want to network with at least 3 new people tonight")

- Jump right into talking to others...don't wait, or else you may never bring yourself to do it. It helps to be a little prepared before going to an event. You can visualize yourself talking to people successfully, have a list prepared of topics to talk about and a reward planned ahead of time for the successful accomplishment of your networking goals.

Health Issues. Since introverts tend to bottle up their feelings, it can often lead to health issues such as extra stress, which can then lead to a slew of other health problems. A good solution to this is just to make sure that you eat right and exercise. Exercising with cardio and strength training methods are great for reducing stress. Other good stress-free activities include yoga and meditation. To learn about some advanced health techniques, please refer to my very popular book: Ultimate Health Secrets.

Feeling Unnoticeable. Another common challenge for introverts is that they may often feel unnoticed. When it comes to this challenge, sometimes it is necessary to practice extroversion. That doesn't mean that you shouldn't be true to yourself—in fact, you should never fight introversion—but most everyone has the ability to be extroverted for short periods of time. Here are some great tips:

- Learn how to mimic characteristics of extroverted people.

- Believe in yourself—the rest often comes naturally.

- Practice engaging in conversation skills whenever you get the chance. If this is something you struggle with, be sure to make better conversation skills a goal and feel free to check out my best-selling book: Communication Skills.

- Pretend like you are an actor playing in a movie.

- Work on building up your confidence and self-esteem to make it easier.

- Make a small effort to be sociable—you'll be surprised to see how much just a little initiative can go a long way!

Finding the "Right" Job. It can be challenging for introverts to find a career that is fitting. In a few chapters, you will discover some great career ideas that may be good for you. In the meantime, here are some tips for fighting workplace challenges:

- Take a personality/aptitude test to see what fields you will excel in. A nice one can be found here from Psychology Today: Career personality/aptitude test.

- Weigh out the requirements of any job you apply to (for example, an introvert would probably not apply to a job that required cold calling or a lot of socializing.)

- Think of what you're knowledgeable in and try to pursue a career in that field. Your career is one of the most important things in your life, so be sure to put a lot of time and effort into finding the right fit for you. Otherwise it can be a depressing and sad life if you're stuck doing something that you hate.

- Don't be afraid to use your creative thinking skills to contribute ideas. This is an area where many introverts excel at, so be sure to let your ideas be known!

- Know your talents and what you're good at doing so that you can make intelligent decisions for long-term prosperity and happiness.

Job Interview Skills. Due to their quiet nature, some introverts dread going on job interviews. The worst part of job interviews for many introverts is trying to answer questions that they have not prepared for. Luckily, there are some great ways to ease the pain of going on a job interview. These tips can also help you ace the interview and get the job.

- Research common interview questions and craft your answers in advance so they're fresh in your head.

- Research your interviewer to build rapport. A good idea is to look at their LinkedIn profile or online company profile.

- Research the company to come up with answers to questions such as, "Why do you want to work for this company?" Also be sure to know what the company stands for and what the company's goals are.

- Think of questions to ask the interviewer beforehand. The interviewer will almost always ask you "what questions do you have for me?" Not asking intelligent questions can make it look like you haven't done any research or that you don't want the job.

Getting Used to Small Talk. There may be nothing more dreaded by introverts than small talk—whether it be at work in the morning, at networking events, at family functions or anywhere else. Many introverts think of small talk as a waste of time, but it happens and is a useful skill to have. Since small talk is many times hard to get out of, you will most likely have to just deal with it. Luckily, there are some easy ways to get through small talk successfully.

- Don't fight it—be curious about others and open to conversation.

- Prepare yourself ahead of time if possible—get into the right mindset.

- Talk about positive things only—no one is interested in negative people.

- Ask all the questions so the extrovert does most of the talking. Being a good listener is a skill that many people value and introverts.

- Read up on current events so you have a shared topic to talk about.

- Just go into it having fun—a positive outlook often means positive results.

Developing Relationships. Finally, developing relationships may be more challenging for introverts than extroverts. Most of it has to do with not being able to engage in small talk—which often leads to more involved relationships. Some introverts may find it hard to talk to and meet people. Some believe that introverts and extroverts cannot date each other because of the stark difference in their personalities and preferences. The truth is that it really depends on the two people and many times introverts and extroverts fit well together in relationships. Here are some great tips on how introverts can develop good relationships:

- Remember, any relationship has to be **healthy** for long-term success.

- Try online dating if you're not sure where to begin. Introverts often find it much easier to chat online first before meeting up.

- For first dates, try things that don't require much talking, such as mountain biking or dancing.

- All in all, be honest with yourself and your partner when it comes to dating, and always try to be nothing but positive on the first three dates.

Learning How to Talk to Others

Although introverts aren't shy, they still often have a harder time making small talk and engaging in conversations with others. The best way to overcome this is to work on your verbal communication skills. You can discover more advanced skills on how to improve your verbal communication skills in my book: Communication Skills, but for now, here are some good starting tips that you can implement into your life to make talking with others easier:

- Make a conscious decision to want to change your conversation habits. The more you are aware that you want to improve your talking skills, the more successful you can be at doing so.

- Set goals for yourself—for example, if you want to become more comfortable talking to strangers, set small short-term goals such as "get comfortable making eye contact" and "get into the habit of starting conversations" (more on this later).

- Eliminate all negative perceptions of talking from your mindset (such as the fact that people may be hard to converse with or that talking with others is meaningless). These negative attitudes can prevent you from improving your verbal communication skills all together. For professional advice on maintaining a great attitude for everyday of your life, be sure to check out my book: Attitude: Discover The True Power Of A Positive Attitude.

- Have an exit plan ready. By doing this, you can feel more secure in ending the conversation whenever you want too. Remind yourself that a short conversation is not the same thing as a bad conversation, and it is always great to leave on a high note along with some quick contact information if desired.

- Have some general conversation topics on hand. Good ideas are to just keep up on the news and local sports, as there's always something interesting to talk about that's current.

- Practice having "contagious" attitudes such as kindness and gratitude as they can help you be more likeable.

- Don't be a perfectionist—tell yourself it's okay to experiment until you get it right. The most successful people in the world are famous for their ability to keep on pressing forward no matter what happens, and just learning from their mistakes as they go.

- Don't try to impress others, just focus on making yourself comfortable.

Chapter 2: Discover Your Special Talent

It seems that for every challenge an introvert faces, he or she has a special talent that makes up for it. Although extroverts seem to be very skilled at being sociable, friendly and successful, it is important to remember that no one person is a master at everything. Though introverts might stumble across many challenges in their lives, there are also lots of things that come as a breeze to them. This chapter will take look at the most common talents of introverts and how you can make the most out of them.

Focus Skills. Introverts are very talented when it comes to focus. While extroverts are easily distracted and may tend to rush things, introverts have a knack for being detail-oriented, persistent and dedicated in their work, whatever it may be. Introverts are less likely to distracted, which helps them shift their focus on the details. The benefit of having great focus skills is that it helps foster deep, long-term relationships. For example, an extroverted salesman may be so focused on closing a sale that he or she focuses more on the deal than the buyers. This can often leave the buyers feeling unappreciated. On the flip side, an introverted salesman may take the time to focus on the buyers and work closely with them in order to give them what they really need and then close the sale. In turn, this can leave the buyers feeling good and more likely to become repeat customers, along with a nice bonus of recommendations to friends and family members. However, if you do have trouble focusing sometimes, my favorite supplement for this is Focus Formula. I use it almost every day and love it.

Decision-Making Skills. Decision-making skills are very useful to have in life because you're going to have to choose between lots of things over the years. Introverts are often better at extroverts at making decisions because they don't jump to conclusions. Instead, introverts allow their brain to process information and they are very cautious in choosing between multiple outcomes. Introverts do this by taking a step back and looking at the bigger picture. They tend to ask more questions to help them come to the most logical decision. Once they have gathered enough information, they weigh it before making a final decision. Some of the greatest chess players that have ever existed were introverts.

Business Relationship Development Skills. Introverts build rapport more easily with their co-workers and counterparts. This is usually because they are good at listening and observing, which allows them to gather and use information to their advantage. Because of this talent, introverts are usually best at managing workplace conflicts. Also, while it can be hard for introverts to develop relationships and friendships, this makes the process a whole lot easier.

Self-Sufficient. Another great talent of introverts is that they are more likely to be self-sufficient. They often like to and are able to work alone, which makes them great managers or leaders. They do not require the supervision of other leaders. Most importantly, this makes introverts less likely to be influenced.

Creative Thinking. Introverts who tap into their inner creative genius are likely to excel in this area. Many famous writers, artists, actors, movie directors and even scientists are introverts. Good examples of famous creative introverts are JK Rowling and Steven Spielberg. However, you don't have to be artsy to be able to consider yourself creative. Think about your hobbies and what you like to do. Often times your hobbies can help you bring out your creative juices. For example, do you like to cook and experiment with different ingredients? That counts as creativity, too.

Listening Skills. Introverts have great listening skills. This is mainly due to several things: introverts don't enjoy multitasking, they are less likely to interrupt and they are good at asking questions to get to the bottom of things. Extroverts often appear as if they are listening, but many times they are thinking about other things, such as what funny thing they should say next. Since introverts are so detail-oriented, you can trust that they're actively listening to you, that's why they make really good best friends.

Leadership Skills. Introverts often make great leaders when they combine all of their talents together—listening, decision-making, creative thinking, focus, and enough extroversion to get the job done. The one challenge is that it is hard for many introverts to get recognize as good leaders because they do shift toward the quiet side while extroverts are loud, outspoken and more likely to get noticed by their supervisors. The bottom line is, no guts no glory. If the introvert is putting out pro-work, they are going to have to stick up for themselves and make sure that they are getting what they deserve. Often time's direct e-mails work great for introverts, as they can fully detail all of their accomplishments and why they should be getting their just rewards!

Reflection Skills. Introverts are good at reflecting, which makes them more likely to learn from their mistakes.

Passion and Expertise. Introverts tend to be passionate and experts at what they do because they have the ability to commit themselves. This gives many introverts a leg up when it comes to qualifying for jobs or just being knowledgeable. It can also serve as a conversation starter in some situations.

Best Types of Jobs For Introverts

Sometimes it can be difficult for introverts to find a fitting career due to their solo nature. Many introverts would hate a job where they have to travel around all day, talking to people, making connections and driving sales. In a world where sales, marketing and other jobs that require extroversion dominate, it can leave introverts feeling drained out and helpless. I can tell you from personal experience, I am definitely an introvert but was also highly successful in sales. It was a good experience to polish my skills, but it was never something I was really passionate about. I was one of the best, so what I enjoyed was beating the whole office or become the employee of the month etc. I also enjoyed the paychecks, but it never really left me fulfilled. I always knew that I was meant to do something else. It took me twenty years before I went back to what I have always been good at since a young age, writing and have a much greater sense of fulfillment in my life. The earlier you can find a career that you're happy with and passionate about, the better your life will be. Here are some great ideas for careers in which introverts tend to excel. The trick is in knowing which one is the right one for you! If you find something that you enjoy, stick to it no matter what and be sure to follow your own heart. This concept is summed up nicely in this great YouTube video: Six Secrets To Success by Arnold Schwarzenegger posted by Travis Fisher.

Animal Care. Many introverts may find themselves drawn to a career in which they work with animals. Animals are very comforting and they do not require small talk or any verbal communication. Good ideas to find jobs in this area would be to check out pet stores, pet shelters, or veterinarian offices. The only drawback is that this field is very low paying. However, you can make a decent amount of money as a trainer or owner.

Historian. Many historians or archivists often work by themselves in museums or auction houses or government buildings and don't deal As much with people as they do with documents and artifacts. The average pay of this field is around $50,000 a year.

Court Reporter. Being a court reporter is the closest you will get to being a fly on the wall. Court reporters may find themselves right in the middle of the action but they don't have to interact with anybody. Instead, they just report what's going on and that's it. The average pay of this field is also $50,000 a year.

Geoscientist. Paying nearly $100,000 a year, this is a perfect job for an introvert who loves to be outside. This job requires very little interaction with others, as most of the time is spent outside or at a computer.

Astronomer. This is another scientific job that would be perfect for introverts. Like a geoscientist, this job can also pay close to $100,000 a year. What could be better than studying the night sky and stars without having to be bothered much?

Social Media Management. This job is becoming more and more common as businesses know that they must utilize social media. This job is perfect for interacting with others through a screen, which many introverts would be comfortable with. The average salary for this job is around $55,000 a year.

Film Editor. If you're really good with editing film or videos, you could land yourself a job in editing. Editing is usually done in a quiet room where you're by yourself. It requires maximum focus and concentration and pays around $50,000 a year.

Medical Records Technician. If you've always wanted to work in the field of medicine, but you're not up to the task of directly dealing with patients all day long, a medical records technician job may be good for you. Instead of having to deal with patients, you will just have to deal with their paperwork. The average pay in this field is around $35,000 a year.

Writer. If you're particularly good with expressing yourself through words, a writing career may be a good fit for you. Technical writers get paid the highest, around $65,000 a year. You could also try to break out as a published author or a freelance writer, although the salary for those two careers can fluctuate based on your success. But writing can be a great source of passive income if you are doing quality work that really helps people.

Entrepreneurship. Since introverts have the ability to work independently, they often have a higher advantage when it comes to building a business. When done right, your own business can set you for life. It is a great way to make money and work comfortably. It isn't always easy, and it may not work on the first try, but if you can get a successful business going it can be one of the most rewarding things you'll ever do.

Chapter 3: Determining Your Personality Type

The Myers-Briggs Type Indicator Personality Test is a means of standardized personality measurement, originally developed by Katherine Briggs and Isabel Myers. The test is based off the research of Carl Jung and aims to clarify the personality theories that he once talked about. Jung originally theorized that peoples' behaviors are consistent despite the fact that they may come off as random and varied. He believed this was due to their judgment and perception. Myers and Briggs developed their test to help make this theory more accessible to the general public.

The Myers-Briggs Type Indicator Personality Test breaks the results down into 4 letters, which are derived from four categories. The categories are "introvert or extrovert," "sensing or intuition," "thinking or feeling," and "judging or perceiving." When people receive the results of taking this test, they get a combination of those labels, which ultimately translates to their personality type. For example, you may get the result of ISTJ while the person next to you could get a result of ENTP. There are 16 Myers-Briggs personality type results:

- ISTJ
- ISTP
- ESTP
- ESTJ

- ISFJ
- ISFP
- ESFP
- ESFJ

- INFJ
- INFP
- ENFP
- ENFJ

- INTJ
- INTP
- ENTP
- ENTJ

According to Myers and Briggs, all types are equal—no one type is better or worse than the other. It costs money to take the actual test but you can take a close variation of it here to see what your type is. This YouTube video, Intro to the Myers-Briggs Personality Test by watchwellcast, provides a light, easy to understand explanation of the different categories.

Knowing what your type is can benefit you in several ways. First, it can help you understand your leadership style—how you might manage others, resolve conflicts, coach others, or otherwise help people in your environment. It can also help you to tackle your own work. Knowing your personality type can also help you effectively manage your time, solve problems, make the best decisions and deal with stress in a healthy manner. Other bonuses include helping you to adapt to new skills, handle change and work better on teams.

In-Depth Descriptions of Myers-Briggs Personality Types

ISTJ. This personality is known as "The Duty Fulfiller." Somebody with this personality type is often a hard, serious and dedicated worker who always achieves his or her goals. People with this personality type are best known for their good focus skills and the desire to live in peace.

ISTP. This personality is known as "The Mechanic." Somebody with this personality type is very good with mechanical skills and always strives to know the "why" of a theory. People with this personality type are best known for being risk-takers who are more likely to ignore rules and laws if they are focused on completing something.

ISFJ. This personality is known as "The Nurturer." Somebody with this personality type is often a dependable person who focuses on the welfare of others. People with this personality type are best known for being quiet and kind to others, with a focus on service.

ISFP. This personality is known as "The Artist." Somebody with this personality type is often non-confrontational and sensitive. People with this personality type tend to be creative and can often see the beauty in something others may not. They are also known to be loyal, loving people.

INFJ. This personality is known as "The Protector." Somebody with this personality type is often moral, individual and committed to their values. People with this personality type are best known for putting others before themselves and can often "read" people well.

INFP. This personality is known as "The Idealist." Somebody with this personality type is often open-minded and reflective. People with this personality type are best known for being excellent writers who enjoy loving and helping others.

INTJ. This personality is known as "The Scientist." Somebody with this personality type is often knowledgeable, analytical and always knows how to turn plans into results. People with this personality type are best known for finding the meaning in something. They are also good leaders.

INTP. This personality is known as "The Thinker." Somebody with this personality type is often creative and knowledgeable yet logical. People with this personality type are best known for thinking of a vision and then making it understandable. They tend to be quiet and it may be difficult to get these types to open up.

ESTP. This personality is known as "The Doer." Somebody with this personality type is often driven for immediate results. People with this personality type are best at working with others who enjoy a risky, fast-paced life.

ESTJ. This personality is known as "The Guardian." Somebody with this personality type is often athletic, organized and moral. People with this personality type are best known for being in charge of things while staying organized and peaceful.

ESFP. This personality is known as "The Performer." Somebody with this personality type is likely to have fun while being around others, hence the name. People with this personality type are best known for living in the moment and always looking for something new to do. They enjoy being the center of attention but do not care much for science or theories.

ESFJ. This personality is known as "The Caregiver." Somebody with this personality type is likely to be confident and warm towards others. People with this personality type are best known for being the responsible ones while putting others before their own needs.

ENFP. This personality is known as "The Inspirer." Somebody with this personality type is often good with people while they come up with exciting ideas. People with this personality type are best known for be exciting and creative. Their interests often fall along a broad spectrum of things.

ENFJ. This personality is known as "The Giver." Somebody with this personality type is often popular due to their excellent people skills. These personality types often hate being by themselves. People with this personality type are best known for being able to see things with a "walk in your shoes" perspective.

ENTP. This personality is known as "The Visionary." Somebody with this personality type is often mentally sharp with a knack for being assertive and eclectic. People with this personality type are best known for being able to easily understand problems and coming up with quick solutions.

ENTJ. This personality is known as "The Executive." Somebody with this personality type is often a natural leader. They are especially skilled at coming up with conflicts to difficult problems. People with this personality type are best known for being well-organized, outspoken public speakers.

Now that you have learned about the details of each personality type on the Myers-Briggs spectrum, which one are you?

Chapter 4: Utilizing Your Inner Strengths

Everyone has inner strengths and talents. The beauty of this is that no two people are alike, so your strengths and talents often make you a unique individual. Discovering your inner strengths normally doesn't happen overnight—it's often a process that you experience as you grow older. There are many reasons why it is important for you to actively figure out what your inner strengths are. The first reason is that if you don't, you may end up wasting your life by doing something that just doesn't suit you. The second reason is that it is difficult to set goals without knowing what you should be focusing on.

Many people never discover their inner strengths because they are too focused on just struggling to get by in life. They may become overworked, stressed out, or unable to focus. The good news is that many people discover their inner strengths by spending time with themselves, which is something that introvert's are highly skilled at doing. Therefore, introverts often have an easier time with this process.

This chapter will help you determine what *your* inner strengths are.

What do you do during your "me" time? Take a moment and think about how you spend time with yourself. Do you like to write, draw, think, read, etc? How you like to enjoy your quiet time can say a lot about what your strengths are. If you spend a lot of time writing, you might have a certain way with words that can win over any reader. If you like to spend a lot of time doodling on scrap paper, you may have the power to paint something that many people can appreciate. Do you like to spend time in nature? You might have a special talent for working with animals. The answer to this question all depends on you. Think about what you do with yourself most often and how you could use it to live a fulfilling life. By taking the time to do this now you can save yourself a lot of pain and aggravation in the future.

Take a Walk Down Memory Lane. Take another moment and think back to your childhood. When you are a child, you usually have no shame in doing what you enjoy, even if you're not "publicly" good at it. For example, maybe you liked to sing a lot but you stopped because you were afraid of others judging you. If you did it as a young child, odds are you might still enjoy it today. It might be a good idea to think about the things you enjoyed doing when you were young and pick them up again. As an adult, you now have the power to shape those activities into something worthwhile and useful.

Ask Others Their Opinion of You. If you truly cannot figure out what your inner strengths are, ask those who are close to you. Sometimes it is easier to get an outside opinion because it is not as biased as if you were analyzing yourself. You may not see something that a close friend or family member may see. For example, you may have a talent for being caring and loyal in times of need but you may not see it because it comes naturally to you. Although this task can be extremely scary and possibly painful, the insight that you will learn can help you for the rest of your life!

Find Your Life's Purpose. Part of finding your inner strengths and talents can be a part of finding your life's purpose. For more information on this, I highly recommend checking my other books: Personal Growth and Ultimate Self-Confidence.

Trust Your Gut. If you feel driven or drawn to something, trust in your instincts and pursue it. This is another popular way that many people discover their inner strengths. Your instincts will often help bring out your passions. Remember, you need to do what makes you happy! Chances are there will be people in your life who will try to dissuade you from following your dreams. Always remember to trust yourself, ignore the naysayers and keep moving forward with your goals and dreams firmly in your mind.

What Doesn't Kill You... Don't focus on anything bad that has happened to you, but instead try to reflect on some circumstances that were challenging but ultimately successful. Figure out what you did to get through those times. Sometimes the strengths that you build after experiencing a challenge can be really powerful. Nobody's life is 100% easy so you are bound to have gone through some challenging circumstances that have made you who you are today.

What Motivates You? Often times, there is something that is pushing you to pursue your strengths, talents, goals and dreams. Many people are motivated by family, values, connections, and money. What's your motivation?

Create an Inspiration Board. One good way to foster your inner strengths is to create an inspiration board—something that you can keep nearby that will remind you about how great you are and what your goals and dreams are that you should be focusing on. This generally includes pictures, quotes, memories, mementos, or anything else that makes you feel happy, motivated and inspired.

Explore Religion/Spirituality. This may not work for everybody, but it may be worth exploring religion and trying to connect with an "authoritative figure" to help find your inner strengths. Some people find comfort in turning to their faith. Good ideas to start exploring this category would be to engage in prayer, meditation or attending a local church.

Aptitude/Strength Tests

Another interesting way to discover your inner strengths are to take some aptitude tests. While there is no saying how accurate these tests really are, it can serve as a useful starting point.

Career Aptitude Test

Verbal Aptitude Test

Numerical Aptitude Test

Mechanical Aptitude Test

Non-Verbal Aptitude Test

Typing Speed Test

Helpful YouTube Videos

Susan Cain Explains How Society Would Benefit From The Strengths of Introverts by Susan Cain

How to Survive a Networking Event as an Introvert by MetteMuller

Never Quit – Good for self-inspiration by MotivationGrid

In Sales, Introverts or Extroverts Win? By Victor Antonio

Leading as an Introvert by Lynda.com

Chapter 5: Making a Plan to Accomplish Your Goals

Now that you know just how great it is to be an introvert, the next and final step is to learn how to put everything together to make the most out of your life. This chapter will use an example to show you just how easy it is to bring everything together and harness the power of being an introvert.

Step 1: Set Your Goals

Whatever your goals are in using your personality to the best of your abilities, the first step above anything is to set goals. A good idea is to set from between 3 to 5 goals for yourself at a time. That way you don't overwhelm yourself to the point where you want to give up. A good idea is to set several short-term goals to help yourself reach a long-term goal. For example, let's pretend that your overall goal is to become more comfortable socializing in large groups of people. You could make one goal to practice working on eye contact and you could make another goal to start learning the best techniques for striking up conversations with others. Your third goal could be to learn how to be more confident in yourself. Notice how each goal nicely transitions into one another—learning eye contact can make it easier to strike up a conversation and the better you get at that, the more likely you are to be confident in yourself.

Step 2: Decide What Talents You Have

Think back to chapter 2. Do any of those talents ring true for you? Take a few moments to look at your goals and see how you can apply any of your introvert talents to help yourself reach those goals. For example, let's pretend that you're really good at listening and focusing. To help yourself achieve each goal, you could put your best focus onto them. Use your listening skills to help reaching each goal easier. For example, you can listen to other people talking first to get an idea about who they are and their interests. Once you've got a comfortable grasp on that, you can look someone in the eyes more easily knowing that you've got a good idea about them. Think about how you could apply other talents to this skill.

Step 3: Plan Ahead For Everything

To reach your goals in the most comfortable manner possible, the best strategy is to plan ahead of time for everything. The more you plan ahead, the more prepared you will feel and the more likely you will be confident and comfortable. For example, if you want to plan ahead for making eye contact with people, you could try practicing in the mirror or practicing with close family members. You can also mentally prepare yourself for the task with positive visualization.

Step 4: Practice Relaxation Techniques

It is normal to feel nervous or anxious when it comes to leaving your comfort zone but you should not let that sole fact hold you back from bringing out the best in yourself. A good idea is to make it a regular habit to practice relaxation techniques to help you prepare yourself for tackling your big goals.

Some people find it helpful to meditate on a daily basis. Here is a really great YouTube video by Rebekah Borucki that can get you started: 3 Ways to Cure Anxiety With Meditation – How To Meditate For Beginners .

Another good way to reduce stress is to practice aromatherapy, which is known to help release stress and help bring about positive moods. You can do aromatherapy yourself at home by simply purchasing a small oil diffuser and some different scents to experiment with. My favorites are lavender, sandalwood and rosemary.

Finally, the best and most natural way to fight anxiety is to schedule in regular exercise. Make sure that you eat a healthy diet; too, as too much sugar and caffeine can affect your health and mood and set you up for failure.

Step 5: Take Action

A goal doesn't become a result until you take some action on it. Once you've followed the previous steps, it is time to start achieving. In the case of the previous example, think about any events that you might go to where you may have to socialize in a large group. This could be a company meeting, a party or a holiday get-together. Do whatever it takes to stay inspired—think about all of the potential friends and relationships you can develop by achieving your goal. Also do whatever it takes to stay motivated. Build up on your self-confidence and remind yourself that it doesn't matter whether you're an introvert or an extrovert—you can do it! Remember, introverts tend to make the very best of friends!

Step 6: Plan Some Solo Time

Congratulations—you've made a great attempt to achieve your goal and you're practicing at mastering it all. The last step is to reward yourself for the hard work you've been doing. Since introverts harness their energy in having some alone time, reward yourself with just that. Take as much time as you need to fill your energy levels back up and then go back to step 1 to set and accomplish some more goals. Be sure to keep improving yourself and striving towards your goals and you will be sure to have a successful and rewarding life!

Conclusion

I hope this book was able to help you to realize how awesome it can be to be an introvert. Whether you are an introvert or an extrovert or somewhere in between, the most important thing to remember is that you are unique, original and awesome. You have amazing talents and now you should have some better ideas of how you can apply them to your life for optimum benefit!

You may initially find it a bit challenging to make friends, develop relationships, sweet talk yourself into that great career or easily engage in small talk. However, you are now armed with all of the best solutions to overcome these situations. Hopefully you were able to recognize some of the great talents of introverts in yourself and begin to develop those talents to the best of your abilities. These talents can help you to tap into your inner strengths and make the most out of your life. If you were able to take the Myers-Briggs personality test, you should now have a better sense of awareness of what your personality is truly like.

The next step is to start setting your goals so that you can stop running from your true self and start being prideful of your introverted personality. Take a few moments and write out 3 to 5 goals that you want to achieve—it can be one long term goal or a series of short-term goals that can help in your overall improvement. Then be sure to focus on what makes you happy and fulfilled. Be sure to pursue your goals and dreams with passion and *to never give up*!

Finally, if you discovered at least one thing that has helped you or that you think would be beneficial to someone else, be sure to take a few seconds to easily post a quick positive review. As an author, your positive feedback is desperately needed. Your highly valuable five star reviews are like a river of golden joy flowing through a sunny forest of mighty trees and beautiful flowers! *To do your good deed in making the world a better place by helping others with your valuable insight, just leave a nice review.*

Thanks and Best of Luck

My Other Books and Audio Books
www.AcesEbooks.com

Peak Performance Books

SUCCESS
SUCCESS STRATEGIES
THE TOP 100 BEST WAYS TO BE SUCCESSFUL

Ace McCloud

Ace McCloud

HABIT
The Top 100 Best Habits
How To Make A Positive Habit Permanent
And How To Break Bad Habits

MOTIVATION
MASTER THE POWER OF MOTIVATION
TO PROPEL YOURSELF TO SUCCESS

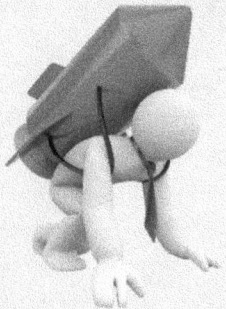

Ace McCloud

ATTITUDE
Discover The True Power Of
A Positive Attitude

Ace McCloud

SELF DISCIPLINE
Unleash The Power Of Self Discipline,
Influence And Willpower In Your Life
To Achieve Anything

Ace McCloud

Competitive Strategies
WINNING STRATEGIES
The Top 100 Best Strategies
For Peak Performance During Competitions

Ace McCloud

Health Books

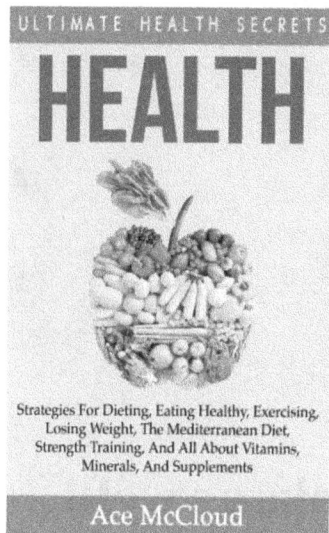

ULTIMATE HEALTH SECRETS

HEALTH

Strategies For Dieting, Eating Healthy, Exercising, Losing Weight, The Mediterranean Diet, Strength Training, And All About Vitamins, Minerals, And Supplements

Ace McCloud

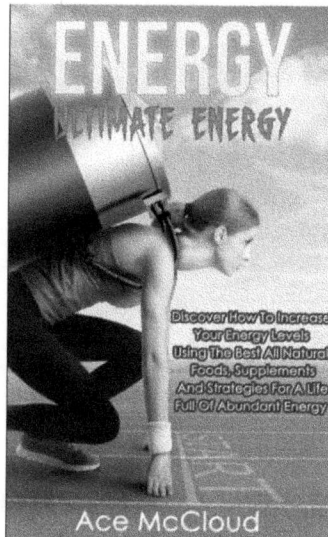

ENERGY
ULTIMATE ENERGY

Discover How To Increase Your Energy Levels Using The Best All Natural Foods, Supplements And Strategies For A Life Full Of Abundant Energy

Ace McCloud

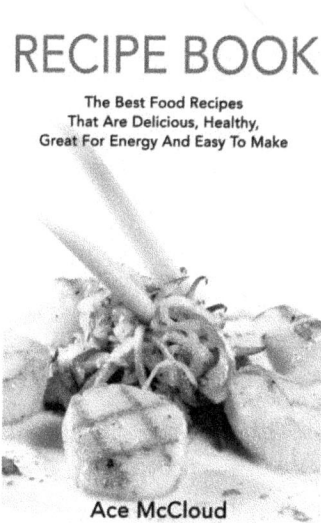

RECIPE BOOK

The Best Food Recipes That Are Delicious, Healthy, Great For Energy And Easy To Make

Ace McCloud

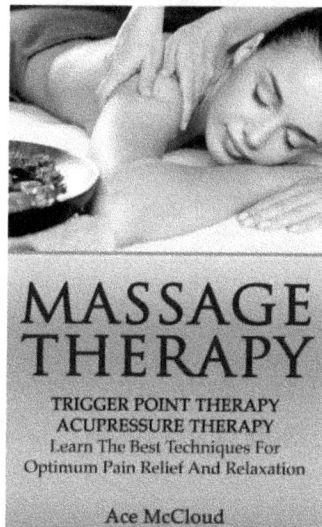

MASSAGE THERAPY

TRIGGER POINT THERAPY
ACUPRESSURE THERAPY
Learn The Best Techniques For Optimum Pain Relief And Relaxation

Ace McCloud

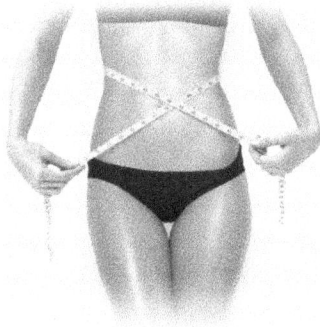

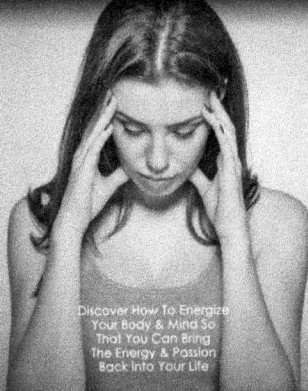

Be sure to check out my audio books as well!

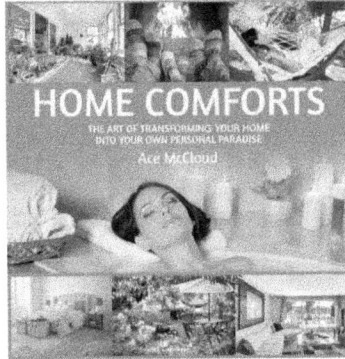

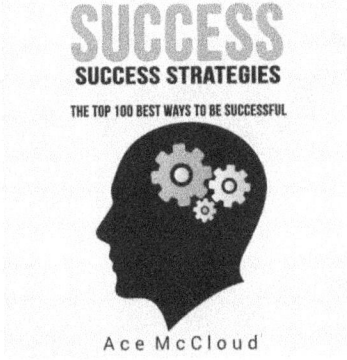

Check out my website at: www.AcesEbooks.com for a complete list of all of my books and high quality audio books. I enjoy bringing you the best knowledge in the world and wish you the best in using this information to make your journey through life better and more enjoyable! **Best of luck to you!**